Unconventional

Classroom

"Flipping the Classroom"

Brent A. Bogan, Ed.S.

Matthew R. Ogles, M.Ed

Published by UCM Management,
P.O. Box 12505
Murfreesboro, TN 37129

http://www.UnconventionalClassroom.com

Published by UCM Management

About the Authors

Brent Bogan is native to the small farming community of Sabina, Ohio. Brent currently resides with his wife and son in Tennessee. Bogan attended Middle Tennessee State University, where he received a Bachelor of Science Degree in Geosciences, A Master of Education Degree in Administration & Supervision, and an Education Specialist Degree with an emphasis in Curriculum and Instruction. In his free time, he enjoys playing guitar, spending time with his family, and traveling. He has been a classroom educator since 2006 and currently serves as a teacher, discipline dean, and the department chair of social studies at the school where he teaches.

Matthew R. Ogles was born in Tennessee and grew up in a small town with small town values. He graduated from Middle Tennessee State University with a Bachelor of Arts Degree in History and with a Masters of Education Degree in Administration and Supervision. He has been an educator in the state of Tennessee since 2008, where he teaches U.S. History, Geography, and World History. His students have consistently had some of the highest growth margins on state mandated tests, while keeping his class exciting and fun. His interests include rock climbing, running, and making music, which he pursues on a daily basis. Matthew and his wife still reside in the beautiful landscapes of Tennessee.

Table of Contents

Introduction

It's that time of year again…new standards. To make things worse, there are more state curriculum standards than ever before! You count the weeks of school, the hours in a day, and you figure something horrible out…you don't have enough time in the school year to cover them all. How on earth can you fit all of the skills into one year, given the limited amount of time you have with the students? The fact is, you honestly can't. Our students are pushed harder than ever to catch up with school systems from other countries that attend school for many more hours per week than the United States. So what exactly is a teacher to do??

Well, for years it has been the same approach to this problem: students enter the room, they sit down, and the teacher lectures a lesson to them. Then, the students are assigned homework and they leave the class. They attempt practice problems or work at home, and then come back to school to try it all again. However, what if a student struggles with the practice work at home? He or she may have time to ask a few questions on the following day; but, for the most part the teacher is ready and all set to move on to the next lesson with minimal time for questions because of a feeling of rushing to cover yearly standards. This causes a problem. The student did not have a full grasp of the first lesson and is expected to build upon that for the second lesson to achieve mastery. This can set the student up for long-term failure. Radical situations call for radical decisions, and one of the most game-changing strategies that has come into education to help with this idea and thought, is "Flipping the Classroom."

This idea allows for the core aspects of the lesson to be taught outside the classroom and for enrichment and guided practice to happen within the classroom. When this is done successfully, there should be plenty of time to cover all the standards and give teachers time to ensure student understanding before moving on. "Flipping the Classroom" is exactly what it says…the students are receiving what is considered the traditional classroom lessons, or direct teaching, outside of class while the practice work is done inside the class under the teacher's guidance. This allows you to check for understanding and to also keep pace with the guides and standards laid before you every year; but more importantly, it allows for every student to achieve mastery. By doing this, a teacher is literally flipping the entire classroom. The benefits to this program are huge in number, so get your notes ready and get your computer, tablet, or cell phone loaded up, because you are getting ready to create the virtual classroom of the future!

Chapter 1

Journey Into the Unknown

Imagine your school being flipped upside down. You're probably visualizing a tornado rampaging through the town knocking cars out of the way as it comes whirling angrily towards your school. As the winds strike your school, the windows begin to break and as the school is pulled from its foundation. The final bursts of wind flip the school upside down and leave it lying on the ground broken, beaten, and worthless. It's a depressing, fearful, and painful thing to imagine; however, when teachers hear the idea of flipping the classroom, that same fear is present. They don't fear for their lives or safety, but they do fear the sense of change. Change is exactly what flipping the classroom is, it is taking everything you do in your lessons and reversing it. Your normal routine and approach will be completely different. Instead of fearing and dreading the change, look at it as an opportunity. An opportunity to reach more students, push more students toward mastery, and to be a leader in the educational world. You are literally creating a classroom of the future, and ultimately that is what the students need, as their world is filled with technology and change.

So what exactly is this classroom of the future? What does it mean to flip a classroom? The best way to understand it is to break it down into two steps. The first step is to take what is traditionally taught during your class time and have students complete those lessons at home. This means your beloved lectures, PowerPoints, videos, and all your student-listening centered lessons must all be completed at home by the students. You are probably thinking, "But, the students need me there to teach them!" While it is true the students do need you to teach them, it is not imperative that you physically have to be there for your lessons. Your lessons can be taught just as well, if not better, through the students' personal computers or phones as a virtual teacher. While this may sound strange, it is much easier than you think! There are tons of ideas and Chapter Two will delve more into exactly how to present your lessons to the students outside of class.

Now vice-versa, the second step of flipping the classroom is taking what is traditionally assigned as practice work, or homework, and having students complete that inside the classroom. You are relinquishing your role as leader on a stage to being a leader by the students' sides. Since the students have your lessons already presented to them virtually at home, class time will include you guiding them through their practice work and assisting them where they need help. The specifics of this strategy will be broken down in Chapter 3.

What the two main steps of flipping the classroom really boil down to is that teachers are just flipping practice and instruction. Teachers are changing what goes on inside and outside of their classroom. When instruction and practice are flipped, you are also changing your role as a teacher. You are going from being the leader at the front of the room to more of a facilitator and tutor to all the students. While the specifics of the students' and teachers' roles will be more clearly defined in the upcoming chapters, it is important to note that it is definitely a departure from the traditional roles on both sides. Although this is something that may be uncomfortable at first, once a teacher begins to see the results in their students' progress and their mastering of difference concepts, it will start to become a normalcy.

When you take these steps, you are embarking on a journey to rework your class and to ultimately construct the classroom of the future. You are taking on the most feared word to the world's population...change. Change is necessary to continuously progress. Will it take some extra preparation? Absolutely! Will it also help students? That answer would be an even bigger, YES! Change is what is necessary for growth! So squash that fear, buckle up, prepare to blaze a path at your school, and get ready to learn exactly how to flip your classroom!

Chapter 2

What Happens Outside the Classroom

Ever since you were a small child, the school system has been the same; the teacher introduces students to a lesson in class and once the student arrives at home, they complete the practice assignment known as homework. This traditional way of thinking about instruction is about to change big time. As mentioned in Chapter One, the idea of flipping the classroom reverses this completely. This means that your lessons must be taught at home... but so many teachers have the same question, "but how?!" It is really far simpler than you ever imagined, you just have to become a virtual teacher through presentations, videos, and online sites.

So let's start with the bare basics, creating a presentation that is available online that every student in your class can access and view as much as they need. The best site to create an interactive and exciting looking presentation is prezi.com. Prezi is an online site that makes creating fun presentations easy. You set the camera views to fly and zoom from one frame to another across a background landscape of your choice, creating an exciting experience for the learner. It is very similar to Power Point, but is more interactive, not linear, and is generally more exciting for the viewer as well. Go to the website and watch some samples to see how entertaining you can make Prezi presentations!

The next big step is deciding what exactly to put inside the Prezi when you create it. Since you are trying to mimic your classroom lessons as closely as possible be sure to include the following ideas in your Prezi: all of your notes from your normal lessons, videos of you teaching the lessons, videos you have found online to enhance your lessons, and pictures of everything you would normally show or discuss in your lesson. You are essentially taking your usual classroom lessons and placing all the details into the Prezi presentation so that students can view them at home and watch them as many times as necessary. Prezi is very user friendly. The site also has wonderful tutorials so the input of photos, notes, examples, or videos should be very easy. There is one part within this process that always trips teachers up though...creating the actual videos of their lessons for students to view.

Creating a video to implement into your Prezi is very simple. If you have a smart phone, you already have an amazing video recorder right at your fingertips. Invest in a tripod and get ready to become a star! The most simple and basic way to record your lessons would be to record yourself teaching the usual lessons in your classroom. While this is effective, just think about all the times during your usual lessons that you wanted to show the students a really cool example that could be utilized with a particular lesson, but when you discovered the example, you were either at home or unable to transport the idea to school. Well, not anymore! You can now record your videos anywhere and easily. You also have the ability to edit them together to create very exciting lessons with many different settings and examples! Let your imagination take over on the videos and just see how nifty you can be!

Once the filming is completed, there are literally hundreds of apps and programs to edit videos. One great app is iMovie. iMovie is extremely user friendly and has a ton of cool features that students will love watching. For example, you can make your lesson videos like movie trailers or music videos! There are several ideas on iMovie that serve as a foundation for your video, enabling you to just copy and paste pictures and videos within the program. It's important to consider making your videos as entertaining as possible, because you want to make the students WANT to watch them. A perfect example of entertainment could be infusing a super hero theme into the lesson. The daily superhero show/lesson could engage students to become involved in the curriculum, while also providing an entertainment value. Students will be talking about the latest episode in the hallways and no student will want to miss out on missing a lesson.

Once the filming and the editing is finished, you simply open Prezi, click "insert video," and then place the video where you want it in your presentation. It is as easy as counting to three. Sometimes it is more effective to make several short videos divided up according to the notes rather than one large video for the whole lesson. The shorter videos allows the student to follow more closely with the notes/pictures, and it also works much better for a student's attention span. Furthermore, the information is easier to digest in short, content rich videos. Students are also more likely to view a shorter five to eight minute video, than a twenty minute video.

While many teachers are comfortable filming themselves, there are many teachers that would prefer to create effective videos where they are not seen. Unless you were a puppet master, this would have seemed like an impossible task…that was until Telegami came along. Telegami is an app where you can create videos with a cartoon version of yourself teaching the lesson. All you have to do is go into the app store, search "Telegami," and click download. It is available in iOS as well as the Android market. Once it is downloaded, the first step is to create a cartoon version of yourself known as an avatar. You can match your usual outfit, hair color, eyes, pants, and honestly just about every aspect of your look! The best part is that the cartoon avatar of me was evidently more dedicated to my diet because he is 20 pounds lighter than me as well! Once your avatar has been created, you choose the background for the particular video lesson that you are teaching. If you are talking about the Andes Mountains, insert a picture of the Andes Mountains as your background. If you are discussing the Pyramids of Egypt, insert the pyramids in as your background! It is often beneficial to have the backgrounds change whenever you swap subjects to help reinforce your lesson.

The next step in Telegami is to record yourself audio wise, teaching the lesson. This is as simple as just speaking into your phone. Make it the appropriate length in regards to your students' attention spans and use an excited, enthusiastic voice, with lots of inflection. If the student can sense you're excited in your voice, then they are more likely to perk up and become receptive to the material. If you are monotone in your audio recordings, you might want to market your lessons as sleep aids for students as another career option. (But you were born to teach so don't do that!) Once the audio is recorded, watch the cartoon avatar move and talk with your voice, teaching your lesson for you! With the avatar teaching in front of the picture backgrounds, it is almost like the students are taking a virtual field trip!

For students who may have hearing impairment, you can type out the captions for the videos you've created. This way, students still have the option to listen, but they can also read everything that you are saying. Once you have created the Telegami video, email it to yourself and upload it into your Prezi through your computer.

While Prezi is our personal favorite choice for interactive presentations for the students, there are other options. Power Point is the program that most teachers still enjoy using prior to becoming familiar with Prezi. You can implement notes, videos, and pictures into Power Point just as easy as Prezi; however, when you have finished it, there is not a database that stores it for you already like Prezi. With Prezi, your students can simply go to Prezi.com and find your presentation. With Power Point you will have to upload the presentation to a webpage for students to view. There are plenty of options when hosting a webpage, such as weebly.com. Weebly is a free website that is very user friendly. Once you have signed up, post your Power Point on your webpage and inform the students of the website address so they can access and view your presentations. Power Points are not the only instructional tools that can be uploaded to a webpage. Prezis can also be uploaded to a webpage and this does have its advantages as well. You can add instructions to go along with the presentations as well as links to assignments or quizzes. Wix.com is another free website builder.

Another advantage to placing the instructional presentations on your website is that students who are absent from school will no longer have to miss out on the lessons from that day in class. They will still have to make up guided practice, but not the instructional lesson itself. Simply have a list of your presentations on your teacher webpage with dates the lesson was assigned. This way students can access the lectures and presentations even if they are ill or have an unforeseen circumstance that prevents them from being able to attend class. Additionally, if students want to go back and review a previous lesson, they have they may do so.

Quizzes are very much an important part of a regular classroom, so it should be of no surprise that it would also be an important part of a virtual classroom as well. The best site to create a virtual quiz for the students is classmarker.com. On this site you register yourself and your students, and then can have students log in and complete the quizzes you have created. It is a wonderful site because you get instant results of how your students perform. You can view results by class, test, category, and so on. The teacher can also see the scores ranked by percent correct, missed, and even the time it took to complete. The teacher can put limits or no limits on how many times the quiz can be taken. Since Flipping the Classroom pushes towards mastery, online quizzes should be used more as practice and we do not personally recommend putting a limit on the number of times they can take it either. The whole objective of teaching is to ensure that the students have comprehended, understand, and have mastered the content. The results of the quizzes can also be exported into an excel file for easy transferring into your gradebook. While this site is free, the number of quizzes you give is limited unless you want to pay money. However, there is another site called testmoz.com that is free. On this site you create the quiz and then it gives you a particular web address for that quiz. Once the students take the quiz, it gives immediate feedback and also sends all the results to your administrator page so you can transfer them to your grade book. The cool features that make classmarker stand out are missing; however, this option is free and serves the basics of what you need for quizzes and tests. The quizzes you create through these sites can easily be embedded into your personal webpage to make your virtual classroom more complete. Finally, three additional websites are Socrative.com, Quizizz, and Schoology.com Socrative and Quizizz are great for creating tests and quizzes. Both sites are free and also have interactive studying games/tools. While Schoology does not currently have the gaming review features, its interface is very user friendly and has multiple options for creating tests and quizzes online, including the ability to have students take quizzes multiple times and having the average of their scores reported for their grade. All three of these options should provide a plethora of alternatives to traditional pencil to paper testing. With so many schools adopting a "bring your own device policy," these websites are sure to help enhance your flipped class and spice up the ways that you engage students into your lessons.

While Weebly is a great options when creating a personal webpage to post your presentations on, there is a secondary option that beats out almost all other webpages for hosting your presentations. This page is called Edmodo.com. This is truly your portal to create the ultimate virtual classroom.

The first thing you will notice about Edmodo once you've created an account is that it looks very similar to Facebook. This is excellent because the students will already be familiar with it and like the format. Once you have followed the step-by-step instructions to create your account, you must create separate class pages for all your classes and individual student logins. Be sure and print a list of all the students' usernames and passwords in case a student loses theirs and needs you to retrieve theirs quickly. Once you have given the students their usernames and passwords, they can log into their class page and see what you have posted for them. On the class wall you as the teacher can make status updates for reminders, cool facts, or best of all your presentations! You can post your Prezis directly onto your classwall for the students to have easy access. Once they view the presentations, they can then post comments on your wall post with questions and comments. Then you can log in and answer all the questions posted. It really is a fully functional virtual classroom because not only are your lessons are there, but you are as well to answer questions.

Edmodo wall posts do not stop with just presentation uploads. You can also post links to quizzes you have created online through the sites such as classmarker.com as well. With Edmodo you have taken the final step in creating that fully functional virtual classroom of the future!

Following all of these steps and creating a virtual classroom will require a great deal of preparation on your part, but it is simple and fun work! Just think…through the presentations, videos, quizzes, and sites like Edmodo, the students can complete your entire daily classroom at home! Plus, what is even better about this compared to your normal classroom is that the students can view these lessons as many times as they need to. In a traditional classroom, the students get one chance to understand the lesson and that's it. In this flipped model, the students get as many chances as they need. This is wonderful because it will lead to greater student mastery of the topics and more educated students in the long run. Once you have implemented the virtual classroom at home for the students, you will never look back.

Are there other sites, steps, or apps you can use to help create your virtual classroom? Absolutely. However, be careful when selecting your way of providing the virtual classroom to the students. You need to make sure the apps, sites, and steps you use are compatible on all types of computers. You do not want a situation where only the windows users in your class can access your virtual classroom. You also do not want the opposite to happen to the Mac users. One extra step that should be considered, is to make sure that every aspect of your virtual classroom can also be accessed on a mobile device. Some students do not have a personal computer of their own, but most do have a smart phone. By making your virtual classroom mobile compatible you also allow the students to complete their lessons on their rides to and from school. It does not stop with just that though, being mobile compatible allows the students to complete their lessons anywhere they go. It is one extra step that allows your classroom to be of greatest convenience to the students. The more convenient it is to the students, the more likely they are to complete the assignments. Every step of the virtual classroom mentioned in this chapter is compatible on all platforms as well as on mobile devices for the students to view.

What happens outside of the classroom is vital to any student's learning. With Flipping the Classroom, the time spent outside of class is used in the most powerful way possible for student mastery.

Chapter 3

What Happens Inside the Classroom

By now, you're probably thinking to yourself, "now that the students are completing the lessons outside of class, I can just kick back, prop my feet up on the desk, and relax during the school day...right??" Wrong. Just because your lessons are taught at home does not mean you can slack during the school day! The role that you play at school, however, is going to be taking a major shift. You are no longer the lecturer of your classroom giving lessons; rather you are now taking on the job of being a facilitator, tutor, and guide to the students. With the lessons taught outside of the classroom, you will now be assisting students in practice work to ensure comprehension of the necessary skills for your class. This chapter is designed to give you ideas of great practice work activities to do with the students inside your classroom.

The first new role you are taking on in the classroom is the role of being a tutor. The practice work you would have assigned to be done at home is now being completed in the classroom with the teacher monitoring student work and checking for understanding. So many students in the past would look at their practice work at home, get confused, have questions, and ultimately just give up because they had no help. The flipped model solves this. The teacher can answer all the questions on practice work immediately when the student works on it during class. Assign the practice work in class and meander your way around the room checking the students for understanding. If a student has a question, stop and help that student gain focus and understanding. It is every struggling child's dream to have their teacher there to help them with their homework.

Being there as a tutor for the students works especially well in math classes. These classes are the ones where the students need the most one-on-one attention to understand steps that build and compound directly onto further concepts. You can read problems aloud to them and help them break down the meaning. You can show students individually how some math steps lead directly to others. As students complete their math practice work, you are there to see where they make mistakes and help the students fix their mistakes. The tutor position of a teacher works in all classes, but it is especially vital to math and science classes.

Practice work should not be mindless worksheets for the students to complete. Now that you are there to help guide the students during practice work, make the assignments more critical thinking oriented. The students will retain the information so much better if they are using higher-order thinking skills. Create their practice work to achieve the upper levels of Bloom's Taxonomy. One excellent practice work to use is Socratic Seminar and incorporating a time for class discussion. This takes the information from the lessons they have completed at home and allows them to think critically about them. Socratic Seminar is an open discussion with the class that is led by the teacher. As the teacher, you will create questions in three different levels for the students. First, you will create questions of clarity. These questions ensure that everyone is on the same level and that they all understood the basics of the lesson before moving on. The next questions should be questions that challenge assumptions. This allows the students to think about what they have learned and form well thought responses as to why they believe certain events or things happen. It pulls on their creativity and problem solving skills. The third type of questions that the teacher should ask the class to discuss should be questions that get the students to find evidence and reasons for their beliefs on the topic. It enables the students to form an argument based upon their opinion. This is the highest level of Bloom's Taxonomy, which is to create a unique thought and to support it. If your state has adopted Common Core, this type of practice lesson is aligned directly with Common Core goals because it supports the idea of critical thinking and searching for evidence. These types of lessons work well in English, Science, and Social Studies classes.

Another example of critical thinking practice work that can be used in the classroom is oral presentations. Since the lessons are completed at home you now have time to allow students to create presentations based upon the subject. Oral presentations should be based upon questions that you give the students. The students should answer the questions based upon lessons, research, and unique thoughts. It allows the student to create, which is once again the highest level of Bloom's Taxonomy. There are two things to be concerned with regarding oral presentations. The first is an underestimation of time. It is vital that students learn to fill the appropriate amount of time without going over because it prepares them for the real world. The second concern with oral presentations is to ensure that the audience is engaged. So many students sit in the audience not listening at all to the other students' presentations because they are nervous about their own presentation. The other half of the students are just laid back after they're believing that their job is done and therefore, they're also not listening. Each teacher should create a category of the student grading rubric to encourage students to find ways to engage their audience. It gets students to be more creative and think critically. This is excellent practice work for your class because it reinforces the lessons they learned at home and pushes critical thinking.

Practice work should also be exciting. It is proven that if students are having fun, then they are more likely to retain the information. An example of a fun practice work is called the Advice Column Lesson. This is a lesson that the students love because it allows them to take on the role of giving advice and essentially being a counselor! Students enjoy swapping roles and by doing this it enables students to have so much fun that they will forget they are still answering assessed questions.

The best way to start this lesson off is to have a sample "Dear counselor" article on the overhead when they come in. You can find these in your daily newspaper. The name of the counselor will vary for each city. Once you have settled your classroom, read the "Dear counselor" article out loud to the classroom...but only the question part! Then get the students to raise their hands and start giving advice on the problem, basically let them play the role of the counselor. Once the students have gone through enough suggestions, show them what the counselor actually said. Then pull up a created question regarding your subject. You will have to stretch your creative muscles on creating the questions, but make up fun and exciting questions related to your curriculum posed from an anonymous person looking for help.

Here is an example:

Dear Counselor,

I have a problem with my troops. I am a young general in the Revolutionary War and I have lost battle, after battle...after battle. My troops are discouraged beyond measure! They don't want to go into war for me anymore and worse yet...they get to quit after one year of service! How can I possibly get them motivated and encouraged enough to enlist for a second year?! Are there places that could possibly be an easy victory to at least get my troops' morale up?!

General in Distress

George Washington

Read through the example "Dear Counselor" questions with the students and get several students to give example answers for the questions to allow the students to know what is expected. Then pass out a questionnaire for the students where all the questions are formatted like this. Allow the students to be creative in their answers and have them answer the questions in letter format as well! The students are assessed on the data and actually have a fun time while completing the lessons! After the students have finished, pull out the best answers from the class and present them! Students like seeing their work presented, it shows what you expect, and it allows you to review over the test material to let students see where they might have gone wrong. Give it a try!

Another exciting practice work is called The Brochure Project. The Brochure Project is a lesson that can be used in every subject. The students really get into this lesson because it allows them to express their creativity while learning at the same time. When finished with a unit or lesson instead of giving the students a normal test, tell the students that you will be having them advertise a specific part of the lesson. For example: In Science, if your class is covering the planets, you could explain to the students that for their assessment they will be given a random planet to create a brochure about. Their job will be to advertise the specific planet and to convince people to want to visit it! Do not tell the students which planet they have until right before the test to ensure that they study all of them. Instruct them to include many different facts about the planet, drawings, and also to throw in creative jokes to make it fun and enjoyable! You should have a sample brochure already finished to show the students as well as a clear rubric to ensure that the work is as educationally sound and clear as possible. The easiest way to create a brochure would be to take a piece of paper, fold it hamburger style and then use it like a normal card.

While this may seem to only hit one subject at a time, it always fulfills ELA standards because creating a brochure allows the students to not only use correct grammar but to also form arguments and understand the use of propaganda in advertisements. So regardless of which subject you are in, be sure to have the students use proper ELA grammar on their brochure. It is a good idea when creating the rubric to just include part of the grade as proper grammar. Cross-curriculum is important because it allows the students to understand how all their subjects relate and are interconnected to one another, as well as to real life and with Flipping the Classroom you are able to implement cross-curriculum lessons into your class more often.

One statement that teachers have always made is that they would "do more group work if they only had the time." Some teacher feel that by the time that they finish the direct instruction of their lesson, there is simply no time left to allow group work. With the flip model and the lessons being done at home, there is now plenty of time to do group work within the class. Group work is an excellent practice work technique because you are essentially allowing peer-to-peer learning. One of the highest levels of learning is modeling and this is exactly what peer-to-peer learning promotes. It allows students to model their learning for other students who might learn best from a peer. It hurts every teacher's self-esteem but sometimes all it takes for a kid to learn a concept is to have their peer teach it to them by using different words and terminology that is more relevant to them. To ensure that peer-to-peer learning is most successful with practice work, every teacher needs to do intentional grouping. In intentional grouping, the teacher purposely matches up the struggling learners with the higher achieving learners. It takes extra effort on the teacher's part, but take your class roster home at night and make your groups out before you come to school to ensure intentional grouping. If students are grouped in this way, then they get a better chance to model their skills and it allows for them to learn from other students. A great app for grouping students is "Team Shake." Team Shake allows teachers to make a list of their high level, mid-level, and low level learners. With team shake, the groups will be created based on various skill levels or can be blended together. Team Shake allows the groups to also change from assignment to assignment, so that students are not always stuck in the same groups.

One group work activity that is always a student favorite is called, the Time Capsule Project! With this practice work the first step is to do intentional grouping, then instruct the students that they will be gathering five items to place into a time capsule that represents that unit/lesson. Instruct them that they will have to present the items in front of the class and have a clear explanation of why the item was included. Create a rubric for this, so the students know exactly what they need to explain. Allow the students to get into their groups and discuss exactly what they need to bring and why. Have capsules (boxes) ready the next day. On that day, have the students present their item, place them into the boxes, and seal the boxes closed. Explain to the students that years from now when a future class covers this lesson that you will pull out their capsule and get students from the current year to figure out why those items are in there! The students LOVE this because it allows them to see their work affecting future students. After the projects have been presented and boxed up, give students their official grades based upon your rubric. This project works great in classes because it reinforces the lesson in a fun and memorable way.

As mentioned earlier if students are having fun, they are more likely to retain information. This applies equally to group work. So now that you have time in class for group work, make the group work assignments fun! Create games for the students to play! One game that students love is called, "Question Tower Topple." First, divide the students up in intentional groups. Then, place a Jenga tower in the center of the room on a table. Then go around to each group and ask them a question from the lesson. If they get it right, they have to remove and replace one Jenga block back on the top of the tower. If they get it wrong, then they have to remove and replace two Jenga blocks on the top of the tower. If the Jenga tower topples on a group, then that group loses! Even when it is not a certain group's turn, they still have to pay attention because if a group misses it, then the same question will be asked of the next group. First, they have to repeat the missed question. If they cannot, then they automatically have to remove 3 Jenga pieces! If they recite the question correctly, then the normal Question Tower Topple rules apply. The game continues until the Jenga topples. The winning team receives a reward! The students enjoy this game and want to win so badly that they will put more effort into studying outside of school lessons in order to not miss questions. The more fun you make practice work, the more likely students are going to really study the lesson because they want to win the practice work challenges. There are literally hundreds of different group review games! In the book, *Unconventional Classroom Management*, there are several more group games described that can take practice work in your class to the next level. Every teacher who does the flip model should be sure to include games in their class time as practice work.

A similar category to group work is hands-on-work. Students love to use their hands and create things. This method can be great for practice work to reinforce the lessons. The classrooms that most commonly use hands-on-work are science classes. So many science teachers want to do labs but never have the time with all the lessons they have to teach. With the flipped model and having the lessons taught at home, there is ample amount of time to do labs in class. Other classes besides science can do hands-on-work as well, but it's up to the creativity of the teacher to determine those lessons.

An unexpected consequence of flipping your classroom is eliminating the amount of papers that you have to grade. As you circulate throughout the room, assisting students in their hands on practice of learning, you can work with students and help assist them to discover the correct answers. If done correctly, the students will have all of the answers to the questions being asked on their in-class assessments, which will reduce the amount grading. It's during this time that you'll be able to check for understanding, versus having to individually grade each and every activity after the end of the school day. This will give you more time to focus on creating the best videos for your students and for grading tests.

The possibilities are endless for great practice work to be done inside your classroom now that the lessons are done at home. It's important to remember that when a teacher is flipping their classroom, their duties as a lecturer at school has taken a backseat. The new role of teachers flipping their class is in the capacity of a tutor and facilitator to get students to learn most effectively. It is a tough seat to take for teachers who love to be the center of attention and the normalcy of how they were taught, but ultimately it is for the best. It will allow the students to push themselves creatively, think critically, and to reinforce their lessons from home because the practice work is done with the teacher present. The goal for any teacher is to push students to their maximum potential and help them to achieve the mastery that every student is capable of.

Chapter 4
For Every Age and Every Grade

There are a vast amount of resources on the internet that gear the flipped classroom towards high school and college aged students. The fact is that all students at every grade can benefit from learning in a "Flipped Classroom" environment. While speaking at professional developments throughout the country, one of the frequent questions that we receive is, "I teach at the elementary school level. Can this work for my students?" The answer is, "most definitely, yes!"

The greatest difference with students at the elementary school level is that it's very difficult to have younger students become fully independent on their at-home lessons. Therefore, it's critical to maintain a direct line of communication with the parents to inform them of upcoming lessons. This will not only help remind students of their responsibility of their at home lesson, but it will also allow parents to stay involved with what is expected of their child in class.

Parents will also need to have more supervision of students while they're online; therefore, parental contact is a must on many levels while utilizing the flipped classroom model for younger students. As more and more schools across America are discovering the success of flipping the classroom and some schools are completely transitioning to this successful model, it will be imperative to allow students to become familiar with this type of schooling early on.

Perhaps the most important part of flipping the classroom at the elementary level is to slowly introduce the concept. At an early age, students are just becoming adjusted to the routine of education and while a full implementation of a flipped classroom may not be realistic for younger students, the introduction of it couldn't take place at a better time. It will be a thing of normalcy when students arrive at middle and high school level if they become familiar with the methods that make a flipped classroom early on.

For years it has been stated that the duration of a lesson should only last for the amount of minutes as the student's age. For example, if a student is nine years old, the lesson should last for nine minutes before a transition is made. This theory should apply when flipping your classroom. The video for elementary school students should be short, entertaining, and to the point.

Since students at this level are still making the adjustments of school at their early age, a complete flipped classroom is not typically feasible. What is a possibility is to give one lesson each week that is a flipped lesson. Discussion will not be as strong at the younger levels, so you could have students fill out a survey, questionnaire, or give them two or three simple questions that corresponds to the video presented. Time can be such an abstract concept for younger children, so a simple introduction may render the best results. We've spoken with teachers who have implemented successful flipped classrooms at the fourth and fifth grade levels, but with that being said; they slowly introduced the flipped classroom to determine what worked best for their students.

Some parents may be against having their students log onto the internet at such an early age. To overcome this potential, but very real hurdle, you could find audio books on C.D. or you could assign individual readings for the students at home. If parents are leery of their children visiting sites, such as YouTube, you could embed videos on your own website.

Teachers can also implement the "flipped classroom" concept by adding learning stations into their classroom for students who need additional enrichment. This is especially a great idea for students who have difficulty finding access to the internet or permission to view videos at home.

Another alternative for students who may not have access to internet at home, or who may not be permitted to use the internet due to their young age, teachers can elect to create DVDs. With bulk lots of blank DVDs available for purchase at electronic stores, it's very simple to use BEP funds to purchase a large amount of DVDs that can be distributed to students who may find the DVDs to be a preferred method of viewing the videos. Teachers can place several lessons on the DVDs and could keep the DVDs at home for weeks at a time, while assigning students specific scenes/chapters to view. Inexpensive flash drives can also be purchased through BEP funds, donations from local businesses, or technology grants. Many students may have gaming devices or televisions that provide a USB port, allowing access to the videos or presentations.

When teachers are facilitators of learning, students have a better chance of reaching mastery of the content. Since lecturing is not a major component of the elementary school level, flipping the classroom at the elementary level helps give students a foundation or background of information on certain topics before it's taught. Teachers can also decide to incorporate the flipped "home" portion of the lesson in the middle of the lesson for continued methods leading to mastery. Instead of doing a complete flipped classroom at the elementary level, teachers can flip certain lessons, especially those where students may have a difficult time grasping a particular concept, such as pre-algebra.

As an increasing number of schools across America are doing complete overhauls and designing their schools to be "flipped schools," implementing a flipped class for elementary level students can only help them for what could possibly be the new evolution of how teachers teach in a school setting.

Chapter 5

Parents

On

Board

You're sitting in your classroom during your planning period and the intercom rings. The secretary asks you to come to the office because you have a phone call from a parent. You make your journey down to the office, hoping to see a parent who just wants to compliment you on a job well done... but deep down, you know the reality. You pick up the phone and just as expected, an upset parent. They have seen their student's grades and want to know why they are so low. They claim that they try to help their child with their homework, but they cannot understand the material themselves. They explain to you that the material is more difficult than what they learned in college! Finally in their last comment, they say, "I want to know exactly what you are teaching in that class." You can explain the lesson to them on the phone, but honestly the only way for the parent to see your lesson would be to come into your classroom, which we all know rarely happens. This parent is clearly upset and not on your side. If this parent had a better understanding of your classroom lesson, then they would be much more likely to be on your side and ultimately help their child succeed more. This is where flipping the classroom comes in.

The number one issue parents have with any teacher is not knowing or understanding the material in the lesson. They cannot help their child with their practice work because they themselves did not see the lesson. With Flipping the Classroom, this is no longer an issue at all. With all the lessons online, the parent can view any of the lessons just as easily as the student. It is a good idea at the beginning of the year to send a note home to every parent explaining how to access the lessons online. This way they can view the lessons and know exactly what is being taught in your classroom. The parents can then watch the lessons with their child and help their child comprehend it better. The practice work is done in class for you to help the student with; therefore, the parent's main job is to help their child understand the lesson you present. Parents love this approach because they are in the circle when it comes to their child's education. They are in the best position possible to help their child study because they get the exact same lesson as their child.

Another key issue that usually comes up in a normal classroom setting between parents and teachers is the lack of communication. Parents often feel the teacher is not communicating with them. With Flipping the Classroom, this problem is solved. Parents know exactly what is being taught, all assignments are online for the parent to see, and all grades are online as well. Programs such as Edmodo also make it where teachers are available for constant communication. If parents or students have a question, they can log into Edmodo and send the teacher an individual message that the teacher can access at home. Flipping the Classroom opens up the lines of communication perfectly for the teacher and the parents.

With the parents now having the ability to help their child as well as having the lines of communication open, the teachers and the parents are essentially on the same team. Often it is a teacher versus parent world, but this concept allows for that wall to be broken. The barrier is taken down because the parent can see what happens in your class and can get in touch with you at any time. It is like when you go to a hibachi grill restaurant and you get to physically see people prepare every bit of your food. You feel more comfortable eating there because you literally watched it being prepared. Parents are the same way with teachers. If they see all of the lessons and how the classroom works, they are much more comfortable and happy with your instruction. You may be thinking, "well a parent should just trust me, I'm the expert." That's a nice idea, but in today's modern society, that is simply not how the education system works in the United States. If we want to get the parents on board, we have to go the extra mile. With Flipping the Classroom, that extra mile is automatically accomplished.

Flipping the Classroom takes away the power of every kid who ever told his parent, "Moooooooooooom, Mr. or Mrs. So and So didn't even teach this and now he or she is going to test us over it..." Now the parents can simply say to them, "Yes they did, we watched his lesson together." This way, they're not already taking sides with their child. Some parents at first may not be supportive of the flipped method, because it's the polar opposite of how they were taught. However, once parents see the benefits and the outcome in the form of better grades, parents begin to see that this new method is something that can benefit their child's comprehension of learning the necessary material. Once parents have become accustomed to the many benefits of the flipped classroom, the model will also provide the backing you need as a teacher from parents, and once you feel that parental support you will never look back.

Chapter 6

Hybrid Flip

Think back to the hottest day of the summer. The sun beating down and the sweat literally dripping from your brow. You are beat. You need something refreshing. Water or a cool glass of sweetened iced tea can do the trick but what you really want is a watermelon. It has everything...water to quench the thirst, melon to satisfy the hunger, and sugar to deliver even the sweetest tooth from evil. As you bite into the watermelon, you notice something is a little hard, you fiddle it around with your tongue and spit it out...it's a seed. That is when it dawns on you; you forgot to get the "seedless" watermelon! Can you still eat and enjoy the original? Absolutely! But would it be better if you had gotten the hybrid watermelon that was seedless? Even more so! You wish you had gotten the hybrid watermelon. Often times when we hear the word hybrid we think of horror or science fiction movies where a mad scientist experiment has gone horribly wrong! In all reality though, the hybrids in our everyday life just make life easier and more enjoyable. So just as the watermelon and lots of foods that we eat benefit from being a hybrid, education can also benefit from what we call, "the hybrid flip."

Let's be honest, several thoughts about Flipping the Classroom may have been running through your mind while reading this book and you may be thinking that perhaps Flipping the Classroom isn't meant for your personal classroom. You're maybe thinking that despite how innovative it sounds, you are not that good with technology. Or you may see the success in your classroom already and think, "why change?" There's probably a small percentage who may think that all of this seems like too much work to take on in one year as a teacher. The fact is that a full flipping of the classroom is not for everyone and some classes will require a great deal more effort, but what we personally recommend in these cases though is at least attempting a hybrid flip. You get the taste of what Flipping the Classroom would be like and see how the students and parents react. You will also find that just implementing some elements of the flip will show immense results as far as student achievement levels. Go ahead and make life easier for you and your students and attempt the hybrid flip!

So what exactly is a hybrid flip? It is simply taking some elements of Flipping the Classroom and implementing them into your teaching. Your lessons will not be exclusively online and your in-class activities won't be exclusively some form of practice work; however, the lines of each will begin to blur.

The easiest way to do a hybrid flip would be to make all of your lessons available online. This will require you to upload all your Prezis or Power Points to a website as described in Chapter 2. Will every Prezi or Power Point have an accompanying video of the lesson? Ideally yes, so the student can review your lesson in its entirety, but at a minimum you should have your presentation from class on there. When doing the hybrid like this, you will still teach the lesson in class, the lessons are merely online so students can re-watch for mastery of concepts. Mastery of concepts is truly the key of Flipping the Classroom and this hybrid method definitely works toward that. Also, by doing this hybrid method it allows for the parents to see what is taught and makes it easier for them to help their child. You reap all the parental benefits described in Chapter 5.

Let's say the biggest thing holding you back from Flipping the Classroom is creating your own lesson videos. You do not care for the idea of having yourself or an avatar of yourself online. Have no fear! As Flipping the Classroom becomes more and more common with other teachers putting their video lessons online, you can easily find videos that align with your own personal lesson to attach to your website or Prezis. The easiest place to look is youtube.com; however, the problem with youtube is that so many schools block it. Therefore, the students who are doing the hybrid flip lessons in the computer lab before or after school can't watch the videos. The best place to search would be teachertube.com or schooltube.com. Both are free websites that have literally hundreds of teacher uploaded video lessons. These are all excellent sources and can greatly expand your uploaded online presentations.

Some teachers take the borrowing one step further and just search and find other teachers' whole presentations and put them on their personal websites. We personally do not recommend this because at that point what you teach in class no longer completely aligns with your online lessons and this can lead to confusion for students and parents alike.

There are websites that specialize in lesson reinforcement. These are sites where you can search for your specific content and find detailed lessons to reinforce and match up with your presentations. The three best that we prefer are Khan Academy, Study Island, and Brain Pop. Khan Academy is a free to join website and it has pre-made lessons on a huge variety of subjects. For the lessons, you can see presentations, videos, and even sample problems. It does have almost all subjects, but its specialty is mathematics. You can search for individual areas in math and add these links to your personal website. The math lessons have detailed videos on how to learn the concept, sample problems with hints available, and even options to show problems worked out. If using Khan Academy in a hybrid classroom, it would be best to teach your normal lesson over the concepts and the make the links to Khan Academy available for the students so they can re-watch the lessons taught on the site. This allows students to work more towards mastery because they have multiple opportunities to understand the lesson.

The same concept applies to the popular site Study Island. Study Island is a paid site, but once your administrators or school board sees the benefits of the program, it's likely that they will find a way to fund the licensing for the site. Study Island works best with grades K-8 and it has individual lessons for all your state standards. This is perfect because once you have covered the lesson in class you can assign students that lesson on Study Island. While the students are accessing the website at home, they can access the lesson and be reinforced on your lesson from class. They can read individual notes and play games with the concepts. This is great for a hybrid class because it is allowing students access to a form of your lesson outside of class which can lead to a greater mastery. You will have to setup an individual student account for every student, but it is worth it because you can track his or her progress.

A third site that helps to implement a hybrid flip is Brain Pop. Brain Pop is an excellent site geared more to K-8. It has fun videos, games, and activities geared to most all subjects. Just search for your topic and then post that link to your personal webpage. This site is less thorough and detailed than Khan Academy and Study Island but it works great to give quick summaries of the material covered in your lessons.

All three of these sites give excellent reinforcements to your lessons. Are they as good as creating your own personal lessons online? Not quite, but it is better than having no way for the student to have a second chance at mastery. These lessons are created by experts and can help the students who just need to hear the lessons a few more times. It will greatly enhance your classroom and student comprehension.

Another excellent program that we were recently introduced to is Ed Puzzle on edpuzzle.com. Although we have not implemented this into our own flipped classrooms yet, we have thoroughly tried the program and it's an all-inclusive tool for Flipping Your Classroom. Ed Puzzle allows you to search for pre-made videos on YouTube, Khan Academy, LearnZillion, CrashCourse, and other fantastic flipping programs.

Of course, it's always better to create your own videos. You want students to become familiar with your style of teaching and your voice. So when creating your own videos, you can upload them onto EdPuzzle, where you can easily crop your videos, add audio voice-overs, and even embed questions within the videos for your students to practice to ensure that they understood the content being delivered. EdPuzzle also allows the teacher to track student understanding.

One easy way to introduce a hybrid flip into your classroom would be to create online study materials for your students. This will allow them to see the concepts of the lesson as many times as they need to, which will lead to greater mastery. A great site that is also an app that goes along with this is Study Blue. On this site you can create interactive flash cards for the students to study and view on their computer or phone. It is just one more way to reinforce your lesson. Students can create their own flash cards on the site as well. Students enjoy it because it is techy, fun, and it leads toward greater mastery. Plus, you'll never have to worry about students losing their index cards in the hallway, because they'll always be in their Study Blue account. Another flash card site that works in a very similar way is called Quizlet. Quizlet functions in nearly the same way except that it is not as mobile based. Both sites allow you to use other teachers' flash cards which works great if you need study material for the students quickly; however, it is much better to create your own because what you deem is important and test-worthy to put on your flash cards, another teacher may have skipped over. You do not want a student studying the wrong or irrelevant material for your concepts. This will only lead to student and parent complaints so we feel it is best to simply create your own interactive flash cards on these sites.

All of the ideas in the book thus far have been on how to get at least some form of your lessons online so students can have a second chance at mastery. This is only half of the hybrid flip. For the second half, you will need to implement some fun and exciting ways to do practice work within your classroom. This way you will fulfill the part of being a tutor and facilitator inside your classroom. Many of the ideas presented in Chapter 3 can easily be implemented into a classroom and for a hybrid flip, we suggest using these practice methods at least two to three days a week. This will allow for students to have an opportunity to ask you questions on practice work, take full advantage of peer-to-peer learning, and have the extra push with group work.

A hybrid flip class is exactly what it sounds like, taking a few elements of Flipping the Classroom and implementing them into your class to strive for better student mastery and academic success.

Chapter 7

Flipping at the University Level

Flipping the Classroom is often branded as being an instructional tool for just the K-12 classroom; however, colleges all across America are beginning to have more and more flipped classrooms. College classes often prefer this method because it allows for more in-depth classroom activities and critical thinking exercises. With the incoming freshman, technology is a huge part of their lives so tapping into it will farther them in the real world even more. If you are an AP teacher in a high school or a professor at a university, you need to know how to flip you classroom.

AP classes and college classes are taught at a much greater depth. The material that is covered is analyzed to a degree that standard and college preparatory classes in high school rarely reach. In order to achieve this level of analytical depth, you as a professor must use the little time you have in class wisely. You can use many of the techniques from Chapter 3 during your class time to reach this depth, but students must truly master the lessons and materials outside of class to keep up. This means that your lessons posted online must be top-notch. In an AP or college class, students handle a longer and more in-depth lesson. In addition to using Edmodo for discussion, Prezis for presentations, and study tools many Universities and AP classes will need to assign textual readings. This is mandatory to reach the scholarly level desired. Most of all reading assignments can still be done online to make it easier for the students to access. With these readings you will still need to offer some commentary or description within your online lessons to ensure students fully comprehend the information. AP class and university class students expect a greater level of depth and it is up to the professor to deliver it to the students and in order to cover the material to that level, Flipping the Classroom is a great catalyst.

Many Universities and high schools are taking Flipping the Classroom to the greatest level and actually doing away with the traditional classroom setting all together; they are teaching purely online classes. With these classes, every aspect of your class is online: lessons, quizzes, discussions, and tests. In many cases, online students are not physically in the same state or region of the university that they're attending. In order to take the lessons to the next level, everything must be done online. The best way to achieve a high yielding learning environment is to create forums or chat rooms for the teacher and students to hold Socratic seminars. A Socratic Seminar will be conducted in the same manner that was described in Chapter 3, but the difference is that the seminar is online in the form of discussion boards. Just because the class is purely online doesn't mean that teachers can't take the students to a greater depth, instructors just have to be inventive and find ways to make the discussions and tutoring available online as well.

Perhaps one of the best benefits of Flipping the Classroom at the college level is that college students have easier access to computer labs, wifi-hotspots, and many purchase other tablets and devices with student loans or an overflow from their scholarships. Flipping the Classroom works great at the university level because students are very motivated when they reach that level. They actually desire critical thinking and in-depth discussions and the best way to give that to the students to help them would be to flip the college classroom.

Chapter 8

Well,

What if...

Whenever a new concept is introduced into the world, it is met with some reluctance. People wonder if the new ideas can really work and they have many questions too. Flipping the Classroom is no different. When this idea was first introduced, the questions began to surface and many wondered if it could actually work. As we have consulted/mentored teachers throughout the United States, we have heard many concerns about Flipping the Classroom, but questions can really fall into five basic questions which can all be easily remedied.

The first question that most educators think of when they hear Flipping the Classroom is, "What if all my students don't have a computer at home?" This is a legitimate concern. While in most areas, over 90% of students do have Internet access either through their phones or computers; there are still some areas where the percentage of students with online capabilities is relatively low. In these areas, Flipping the Classroom can still work though. The students can complete their online work directly before or after school hours. Most schools allow for students to enter the building 30 minutes to an hour before the day starts, and students often wait on buses at the close of the day for up to 30 minutes as well. This can add up to an hour and a half a student is at school with free time. Many schools we have talked with have opened up their computer labs during this time. Students who do not have online access at home, can use the computer lab to complete their lessons. Most schools have a study hall or enrichment time during the day for at least 45 minutes. The students, who do not have online access at home, can use the school computers to complete lessons during those times. What it all comes down to is that there is more than enough time for students to complete their lessons during the school day if they do not have online capabilities at home.

The second biggest question is "What if the student just doesn't do their lessons?" To some degree this has always been a problem with school in general, students not doing their assigned work at home. This is usually handled in a regular classroom by giving grades on homework. This can just as easily be done with Flipping the Classroom. On many sites mentioned in this book, readers can actually see how much time students spent on their online lessons. As a teacher, set a minimum lesson time that a student is required to be actively logged into Schoology, Edmodo, or other site that you utilize to flip your class and include that as a grade. Another idea is to use Classmarker, which was mentioned in Chapter 2, and have students complete quizzes over the lessons for grades to ensure that they complete their assignments. Tying it back to the incentive of receiving a grade will bring the majority of students into cooperation and seeing their progress; however, there is one technique that can have an even greater success rate for an even greater number of students. This method is a proactive method. Making your lessons exciting and engaging enough that students will WANT to do them because they enjoy them. It is far easier than you think with your videos and presentations! Put jokes and energy into them and be creative! To get them hooked, take a few days in class allowing students to complete their online lessons. Once the students realize how much they like them, they will voluntarily complete them. If your Flipping the Classroom lessons are boring, students won't want to do them and you can get their cooperation through grades, but you'll see far greater results if you focus on the proactive method.

When we interviewed a teacher who flips their classroom, she said that she makes students who fail to find time to watch the instructional videos at home, watch videos in her classroom while other students get hands on instruction. Towards the beginning of the school year, she makes sure that her lessons are extra exciting so that students will gain the extra motivation to view the videos. In her classroom, there are five student computers. Students who fail to find a way to view the presentations prior to class, will be forced to do so on the day of practice in class. Those students will have a separate activity from the rest of the class, since they will be behind everyone else. To avoid this exclusion, students work hard to ensure that they view her short instructional videos. If they lack an internet connection at home or any other way to access the videos at home, this could mean going to the school library early in the morning once their bus arrives or asking a teacher in another class to use a teacher if they finish a test early or have five minutes of extra time available in another class. She also mentioned that in the past, approximately 60% of her students would complete their homework. After she began flipping the classroom, there may be two to three students per class who now fail to complete the out of class assignments.

The next common question is, "Isn't Flipping the Classroom putting too much outside work on the students? Kids can't work all the time!" Many people have the misconception that completing the lessons at home will take hours and hours for students to complete. Each class lesson should be about 10-20 minutes in length with younger grades having lessons around 5 minutes in length. With many schools having block scheduling, that means students will usually only have three classes to prepare for each night. That is only one hour of homework nightly. In traditional classrooms, homework is usually much more than 10-20 minutes per class and that is not taking into account all the time used attempting to go through the lesson in the book to just complete the homework. All the parents and students that we've talked to who have actually done the Flipped classroom all agree that the homework load is MUCH lighter in the flipped model.

There are some teachers who stress more about themselves when they hear of the Flipped Classroom. Their question is, "How am I supposed to have time to construct these online lessons, plan exciting activities, and do all my other work??" It is no secret that a flipped classroom requires a great deal of effort. You will have to spend hours in planning the first year that you implement it. However, think about the second year, third year, and so on. All of the planning and creation is done so those years will be very relaxing for you. It's recommended to use planning periods at school to build lessons and use part of a summer break to get started. If the full flip seems like too much work for one year, then refer to Chapter 6 and do the hybrid flip! Once a teacher sees the results with the hybrid flip, they can take the full plunge and do the planning for the full flip the next year!

The final general question that we're often asked is: "With all this push toward online teaching and learning, aren't you afraid students will lose touch with reality?" Technology is the future, we need to train our students to function in the real world that they live in. In the job market today, almost every position requires that people become educated in technology, and the majority of jobs even require that applicants apply on a computer. Flipping the Classroom helps get students ready for their personal future. Also, one hour a day online for lessons is just that, one hour. This is not enough for a student to lose touch with reality. If anything, Flipping the Classroom helps prepare students for their reality.

Flipping the Classroom does bring many questions with it; however, with some reasoning, these questions can be resolved and can be implemented into your classroom. The students will thank you, parents will thank you, and once you see the results, you will thank yourself.

Chapter 9

Does Flipping the Classroom Actually Work???

The Proof.

When it comes to new concepts, people are always asking, "Well, does Flipping the Classroom actually work??" People want to see results before they try something new to make sure that it actually works. Many want firsthand accounts, while others want hardcore statistical information. Flipping the Classroom is not some flash in the pan concept and it has definitely yielded results for those who have tried it. This chapter will explore why Flipping the Classroom shows results, first hand accounts from students, parents, and teachers, and statistical information that can convince even the most skeptical teachers.

Flipping the Classroom shows results when it comes to test scores for one basic reason; it focuses on student mastery. In the Flipping the Classroom model, students can review a lesson as many times as they need to. There is not a one chance try, like you would see in a traditional classroom. Students can view your personal lessons multiple times, and can even go back to past lessons to remember old concepts or catch up. If a student is absent, they also never have to miss a lesson. There is essentially no way for a student to ever miss a lesson again, they are ALWAYS available to them. It is because of this, students are able to fully master concepts. Students essentially get to learn at their own pace until they have mastered the concepts. In the classroom itself, Flipping the Classroom pushes for critical thinking and allows for the teacher to be there to answer questions and tutor on practice work. It opens the door for the best use of time with students. Lessons are mastered at home; therefore, it allows for extra reinforcement in the class through group work, peer-to-peer learning, and individual tutoring. Every student should be able to get the help and attention they need…and deserve. Flipping the Classroom is one of the only teaching styles that pushes towards this full mastery idea. It is because of this concept, student's test scores do increase. They are comprehending the content better and therefore, being able to answer more questions correct on tests.

But outside of just test scores, it also makes these students more ready for the real world and college bound.

Unconventional Classroom is a consultant organization for teachers; as we have traveled to different parts of the United States we have heard many first-hand accounts from teachers of just how well Flipping the Classroom has worked in their classes. Every teacher who has actually put Flipping the Classroom into practice has said nothing but positive things. They speak of how the ability to have the lessons mastered at home has opened so many doors as to what can be done during class time. Science teachers love it because they can do labs, and Social Studies teachers love it because they can do more primary source lessons during class. Teachers of all subjects who have tried it, have enjoyed it because they feel that it frees up the time that they have with the students to actually help them, rather than just rushing through a lesson.

Along with the teachers seeing and feeling results. students feel the same way. The students of a flipped classroom, who we have heard from, have only positive comments to say. The students enjoy and see the benefits of having the lessons available at home. They like being able to go at their own pace and being able to go back if they need to during the lesson. They also report enjoying their classes more because they have more hands-on activities during the lessons. It is well known that if the students are enjoying the lesson and having fun, then they are much more likely to retain the information. They also report that the lessons at home make the homework load easier. They spend less time struggling to remember and understand concepts because the lessons are always there, and this ultimately leads to less time spent on homework because there is greater understanding and mastery. In the old model, practice work could take hours because one had to try and figure out the lesson and then still had to attempt to complete the work. With the flipped classroom model, lessons are easy to understand because students can be viewed multiple times and at the student's own pace. This ultimately takes less time than traditional homework and what student would ever object to less homework?? Students enjoy seeing their class taking advantage of technology. They know that their world revolves around technology and they enjoy being able to see how school work relates to the real world. Overall, the students' opinion is definitely in favor of Flipping the Classroom, and they see the benefits for their own education.

Parents are in the same boat as the students and teachers. The parents we have talked to are in favor of Flipping the Classroom. Parents enjoy the fact that it works for student mastery and class time being used more wisely, but the number one thing that parents like most, is how it opens up the lines of communication between themselves and the teachers. They feel as if they are fully on the same page and working together. Parents are fans of the idea that they can watch the lesson with their kids and can truly help them study because they can see the same lesson. Oddly enough, most parents have embraced the idea that Flipping the Classroom homework takes less time. They see their child less stressed in general, and this makes life easier for everyone. To date, we have not met one parent who was against the Flipping the Classroom idea after they had fully tried it and understood the ultimate goal behind it.

Regardless of why Flipping the Classroom should work or first-hand accounts, what really proves it works is statistics. The best place to look for these statistics is Clintondale High School in Detroit, Michigan. While many schools replicate similar results and high patterns of improvement, Clintondale High School has been the poster school for the Flipping the Classroom. Clintondale High School was by definition a failing school. They had over a 40% fail rate in all core subjects except Social Studies, which was nearly a 30% fail rate. The graduation rate was below 80% and of the ones who did graduate, only 60% of them even attempted to go to college. Clintondale High School was in dire straights. That was until their current principal took over. He had tried Flipping the Classroom with his coaching and had seen results with his team. He therefore decided to get his regular classrooms to try the same concept…all at once. That's right, in 2001 the principal required every teacher to do a full flip of the classroom, and the results for the school were phenomenal. After just one year of trying Flipping the Classroom fail rate in all core subjects dropped to 20 to 30 percent. People usually say math is the most difficult subject to get struggling students to improve in, but the math fail rate at Clintondale High School dropped over 30% in that first year. That is nearly unheard of. After that first year of Flipping the Classroom, their graduation rate hit nearly 90% and of those graduating, roughly 80% went on to college. Most people or schools think it takes years and years to change test scores this much, but Clintondale High School did it in one year. It's owed mainly to one practice, Flipping the Classroom. The test results prove it, Flipping the Classroom works more toward student mastery and does produce results. Other teachers who we've spoken with admit to double digit gains on student achievement.

Are there ways that will not show results though? Sadly, yes, but it is entirely up to the teacher. If the teacher has poor lessons and poor types of practice work, will simply flipping these two make either better? No. Flipping the Classroom like any other method of teaching requires teachers to create great lessons and great practice work assignments. If you already have great lessons and great practice work assignments, will Flipping the Classroom help you and your students? To this, the answer is definitely yes.

Whether it is statistical information, first hand accounts, or reasoning alone, Flipping the Classroom clearly creates results in almost every classroom that tries it. The results are mirrored and replicated for schools who have tried a complete overhaul of flipping classrooms and to those individual classes that have taken the plunge and implemented the flipped classroom strategies. Not only will it create a better and more successful year for you, but parents and students alike will thank you. Not to mention, your administrators will too when he or she sees your results in the numbers.

Chapter 10

Being a Leader in Your School

Being a leader in any circumstance takes courage. A leader looks at change and welcomes it to see if they can make what is already great, a little bit better. A leader is willing to stand out to try and make a difference. You may be thinking, "I'm just not leader material!" Well, every leader has to start somewhere so take that first step today. Let's look at the story of Dick Fosbury to see this in action.

Dick Fosbury was a typical kid from the west coast. He had a love for sports and at a tall six foot, four inches, it would seem that basketball would have been a perfect fit for Fosbury, but he had little success at playing basketball. Fosbury tried his hand at football with another failed attempt at success. It was on the infield of the track at Medford High School in Oregon where Fosbury achieved his athletic success at the high jump.

When Fosbury was in high school, there were two standard ways of clearing the bar during the high jump. The first was called the scissor jump, which involved an athlete taking a running start and throwing one leg over the bar and then the other before landing on their feet. The other method was called the western roll (think of superman flying over a bar) with an athlete's arms and legs crossing over the bar first.

Fosbury wasn't great at either of the methods to clear the bar on the high jump. One day, he tried his own method that involved lifting his hips to help clear the bar. As ridiculous as the jump looked, Fosbury improved his best jump by an astounding six inches. This new method was the beginning of Dick Fosbury's greatness. In 1967, he tried out for the Olympics and barely brushed by to qualify for a spot to compete. He was by no means expected to do well.

In 1968, the Olympics were held in Mexico. A very large crowd started to take notice at Fosbury's unique style of high jumping, which would later become dubbed as, "the Fosbury Flop." While the crowd found humor in his technique, Fosbury had the final laugh by taking home the gold medal and breaking the world record at a jump of 7 feet, 4.5 inches. To this day, high jumpers around the world emulate the Fosbury Flop technique.

Just as people laughed and made fun of the technique that Dick Fosbury used to jump over the high bar, some people may scoff at the idea of a flipped classroom. Everyone thought that Fosbury's jump was a novelty idea that would never work, as many people may view the flipped classroom in a similar manner. Just as something as unconventional as the Fosbury Flop turned into a success that totally changed the standard and method of how the high jump was approached, he reached gold medal success, and flipping the classroom can also have a similar success for test scores and learning outcomes in your classroom. Best practices are ever evolving in all aspects of society and our world, just as they will always change in education. As statistics have proven, the flipped classroom is the new revolution of teaching and learning.

Therefore, we suggest you embrace the changes that are constantly coming your way and stand up and be that teacher at your school who teaches different than the normal way. Will other teachers potentially mock you or the new style? Probably, but only because they don't have the courage to be different and take chances. Change is necessary for improvement in all aspects of life. When we started flipping our classes at our school, there were critics, but when teachers began to see the results, suddenly we were showing other teachers how to do the very same things for their classrooms. You can blaze a path through your school with the highest student success rates, and you will be known as a pioneer. Take the first step, adopt Flipping the Classroom for your students, and be that leader at your school that everyone else will one day model themselves after.